MONSTER MADNESS

THE STORY OF

THE MINOTAUR

ANNA COLLINS

T0002187

Enslow PUBLISHING

Please visit our website, www.enslow.com. For a free color catalog of all our high-quality books, call toll free 1-800-398-2504 or fax 1-877-980-4454.

Library of Congress Cataloging-in-Publication Data
Names: Collins, Anna.
Title: The story of the Minotaur / Anna Collins.
Description: New York : Enslow Publishing, 2023. | Series: Monster madness | Includes glossary and index.
Identifiers: ISBN 9781978531802 (pbk.) | ISBN 9781978531826 (library bound) | ISBN 9781978531819 (6pack) | ISBN 9781978531833 (ebook)
Subjects: LCSH: Minotaur (Greek mythological character)–Juvenile literature. | Theseus, King of Athens–Juvenile literature.
Classification: LCC BL820.M63 C65 2023 | DDC 398.20938'01–dc23

Published in 2023 by
Enslow Publishing
29 E. 21st Street
New York, NY 10010

Copyright © 2023 Enslow Publishing

Designer: Tanya Dellaccio
Editor: Jennifer Lombardo

Photo credits: Cover bogadeva1983/Shutterstock.com; p. 5 iuliia_n/Shutterstock.com; p. 7 (Posiedon) cpaulfell/Shutterstock.com; p. 7 (Pasiphae) https://upload.wikimedia.org/wikipedia/commons/c/c9/Pasiphae.jpg; p. 8 https://upload.wikimedia.org/wikipedia/commons/7/7d/Pasiphae_and_the_baby_Minotaur,_red-figure_kylix_found_at_Etruscan_Vulci,_4th_century_BC,_Cabinet_des_Médailles,_Paris_(22614392466).jpg; p. 9 Derick D Miller/Shutterstock.com; p. 11 (maze) Naypong Studio/Shutterstock.com; p. 11 (labryinth) zayatsphoto/Shutterstock.com; p. 13 Sven Hansche/Shutterstock.com; p. 15 (painting) Science History Images/Alamy Images; p. 15 (statue) olgalngs/Shutterstock.com; p. 17 (Bacchus and Ariadne) FineArt/Alamy Images; p. 17 (Dionysus) Hoika Mikhail/Shutterstock.com; p. 19 PHOTOCREO Michal Bednarek/Shutterstock.com; p. 21 (map) Peter Hermes Furian/Shutterstock.com; p. 21 (coin) https://upload.wikimedia.org/wikipedia/commons/a/a5/001-knossos-01.jpg.

All rights reserved. No part of this book may be reproduced in any form without permission in writing from the publisher, except by a reviewer.

Printed in the United States of America

Some of the images in this book illustrate individuals who are models. The depictions do not imply actual situations or events.

CPSIA compliance information: Batch #CSENS23: For further information contact Enslow Publishing, New York, New York, at 1-800-398-2504.

Find us on

CONTENTS

Boldface words appear in the glossary.

AN OLD STORY

The **myth** of the Minotaur is one of the oldest stories in history. A group of people called the Minoans lived on the island of Crete in Greece between 2700 and 1450 BCE. They're gone now, but this myth is still around.

The story starts with Minos, the ruler of Crete. He made himself king when his stepfather, the old king, died. Minos's brothers said they weren't sure Minos had the right to do that. Minos said the gods wanted him to be king, and he'd prove it.

PEOPLE CAN STILL VISIT
THE RUINS OF THE MINOAN
PALACE ON CRETE.

BELIEVE IT OR NOT!

PEOPLE WHO STUDY HISTORY NAMED THE MINOANS AFTER MINOS. WE DON'T ACTUALLY KNOW WHAT THEY CALLED THEMSELVES! WE'RE ALSO NOT SURE WHETHER MINOS EVER EXISTED. HE MIGHT JUST BE A STORY. MINOS MIGHT EVEN BE THE TITLE MINOAN RULERS USED INSTEAD OF KING.

POSEIDON HELPS AND HURTS

Minos prayed to Poseidon, the god of the sea, for a sign that he was meant to rule. Poseidon sent Minos a bull from the sea. It proved to Minos's brothers that he had the right to be king! Minos was supposed to **sacrifice** it to Poseidon to show his thanks. Instead, he kept it and sacrificed one that wasn't as nice.

Poseidon was very angry that Minos went back on his promise. To **punish** him, he made Minos's wife, Pasiphae, fall in love with the bull.

THIS PICTURE SHOWS POSEIDON SURROUNDED BY SEA CREATURES.

PASIPHAE IS JUST ONE EXAMPLE OF HOW THE GODS CONTROLLED HUMANS' FEELINGS AND ACTIONS IN GREEK MYTHS.

THE BIRTH OF THE MINOTAUR

Pasiphae wanted Poseidon's bull to love her back. She asked a man named Daedalus to help her. He built a wooden cow that Pasiphae used to trick the bull into thinking she was also a cow. She gave birth to a son that looked like a human with the head of a bull.

Pasiphae named her son Asterion after Minos's stepfather, but everyone called him the Minotaur. In Greek, "taurus" means "bull," so Minotaur means "bull of Minos." Everyone was scared of the Minotaur because it ate people!

TO PUNISH DAEDALUS FOR HELPING PASIPHAE, MINOS MADE HIM AND HIS SON, ICARUS, BUILD A LABYRINTH, OR MAZE, AS A PRISON FOR THE MINOTAUR. IT WAS TOO CONFUSING FOR THE MINOTAUR TO ESCAPE FROM. THIS IS THE OLDEST RECORDED LABYRINTH IN HISTORY.

THIS ANCIENT ROMAN **MOSAIC** SHOWS THE MINOTAUR INSIDE A LABYRINTH.

LABYRINTH OR MAZE?

Many people use the words "labyrinth" and "maze" to mean the same thing, but they're actually different! A labyrinth has one curving path to the center and back, so it's impossible to get lost in. It's sometimes drawn on the ground. People often use them for **meditation**.

A maze is more like a puzzle, with confusing dead ends and high walls. The way the Minotaur's labyrinth is **described** makes it sound more like a maze, but that word wasn't invented until long after the myth was written.

LABYRINTH

MAZE

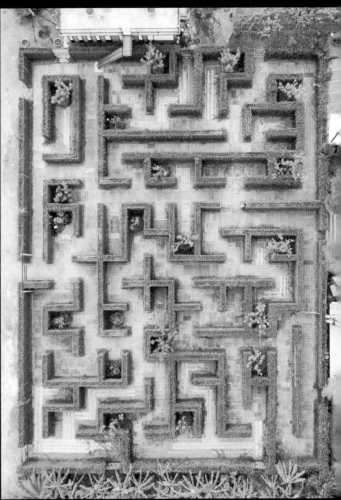

A LABYRINTH AND A MAZE ARE TWO DIFFERENT THINGS.

BELIEVE IT OR NOT!

MANY PEOPLE LOVE MAZES AND LABYRINTHS! *LABYRINTH* IS A FAMOUS MOVIE FROM 1986, BUT IT'S ABOUT A MAZE. PEOPLE ALSO MAKE REAL-LIFE MAZES FOR FUN. THERE ARE REAL MAZES AND LABYRINTHS YOU CAN VISIT ALL OVER THE WORLD.

A SACRIFICE OF ATHENIANS

Minos and Pasiphae had an older son named Androgeos. He went to the Greek city of Athens to enter a **competition**. He won much more than the Athenians did, which made them mad. In one **version** of the Minotaur story, the Athenian king took **revenge** on Androgeos by sending him to kill the bull that was the Minotaur's father. Instead, the bull killed him.

In another version, the Athenians killed Androgeos themselves in revenge. In both versions, Minos punished the Athenians by forcing them to send their children to Crete.

12

AFTER THE MINOANS DISAPPEARED, ATHENS GREW MORE POWERFUL.

BELIEVE IT OR NOT!

THE ATHENIANS' PUNISHMENT WAS TO SEND SEVEN GIRLS AND SEVEN BOYS TO THE LABYRINTH TO FEED THE MINOTAUR. IN SOME VERSIONS, THIS WAS DONE EVERY YEAR. IN OTHERS, IT WAS EVERY NINE YEARS.

THESEUS AND ARIADNE

The third time the Athenians had to send their children to Crete, the king's son, Theseus, said he wanted to be one of them. He said he could kill the Minotaur so no one else would have to be sacrificed.

On Crete, Theseus met Minos's daughters, Ariadne and Phaedra. They both fell in love with Theseus. Ariadne asked Daedalus to help her save Theseus, so Daedalus told Ariadne to give Theseus a ball of string. If he tied one end to the labyrinth entrance, he could follow it back there when he was ready to leave.

THE SUN'S HEAT MELTED THE WAX ON ICARUS'S WINGS.

PEOPLE USE THE MYTH OF ICARUS TO REMIND OTHERS TO LISTEN TO WARNINGS.

BELIEVE IT OR NOT!

MINOS HAD DAEDALUS AND ICARUS LOCKED UP FOR TELLING ARIADNE ABOUT THE STRING. THEY ESCAPED FROM THEIR PRISON BY BUILDING WINGS OUT OF WAX AND FEATHERS. DAEDALUS WARNED ICARUS NOT TO FLY TOO CLOSE TO THE SUN, BUT HE DIDN'T LISTEN.

FIGHTING THE MINOTAUR

Theseus went into the labyrinth and found the Minotaur in the furthest corner. One version of the story says he killed the Minotaur by punching him very hard. Another says Ariadne gave him a sword, and he used that to kill the Minotaur.

When the Minotaur was dead, Theseus followed the string out of the labyrinth. He set sail back to Athens with Ariadne and Phaedra. On the way home, he stopped at an island and left Ariadne there. Even though Ariadne saved his life, he wanted to marry Phaedra.

DIONYSUS

THIS PAINTING SHOWS ARIADNE (*RIGHT*) AND DIONYSUS (*LEFT*), WHOSE ROMAN NAME IS BACCHUS.

BELIEVE IT OR NOT!

THE GOD DIONYSUS FOUND ARIADNE ON THE ISLAND AND MARRIED HER. IN ONE VERSION OF THE STORY, DIONYSUS SAW ARIADNE ON THE SHIP AND ORDERED THESEUS TO LEAVE HER ON THE ISLAND SO DIONYSUS COULD MARRY HER.

A SAD MISTAKE

Before Theseus left for Crete, he and his father came up with a code. The sails on his ship were black. They agreed that if he survived the labyrinth, he'd swap them for white sails.

After leaving Ariadne behind, Theseus was excited to get home to Athens. However, he forgot about the sails. His father saw the ship with black sails from far away and thought Theseus was dead. He was so sad that he jumped off a cliff into the sea. Theseus became king of Athens in his place.

THERE ARE MANY ROCKY
CLIFFS ON THE AEGEAN SEA.

BELIEVE IT OR NOT!

THE ANCIENT GREEKS USED MYTHS TO
EXPLAIN THE WORLD AROUND THEM.
THESEUS'S FATHER WAS NAMED AEGEUS.
THIS IS HOW THE GREEKS EXPLAINED WHY
THE BODY OF WATER WHERE HE DIED IS
CALLED THE AEGEAN SEA.

A BIT OF TRUTH

Because the Greeks used myths to explain their world, there's often a bit of truth in their stories. It's unlikely there was a bull-headed man living in ancient Crete, but maybe there was a real labyrinth!

The ruins of Minos's palace, which is called Knossos, still stand on Crete. There are a lot of hallways, staircases, and twisty passages. For this reason, some people think the the palace was the **inspiration** for the labyrinth. Others think the real inspiration was the Labyrinthos Caves, a **quarry** about 20 miles (32 km) from the palace.

WHERE IS THE LABYRINTH?

CRETE

KNOSSOS •

• LABYRINTHOS
CAVES

KNOSSOS AND THE
LABYRINTHOS CAVES ARE THE
TWO MOST LIKELY INSPIRATIONS
FOR THE LABYRINTH.

BELIEVE IT OR NOT!

SOME PEOPLE THINK THE LABYRINTH IS JUST
PART OF A STORY AND THAT TRYING TO FIND IT
IS LIKE TRYING TO FIND NEVERLAND. OTHERS
SAY THERE'S EVIDENCE TO SHOW THAT IT
COULD HAVE EXISTED. FOR EXAMPLE, SOME
OLD GREEK COINS HAVE LABYRINTHS ON THEM.

GLOSSARY

competition: An event in which people try to win.

describe: To write or tell about.

inspiration: Something that moves someone to act, create, or feel an emotion.

meditation: The act or process of spending time in quiet thought.

mosaic: A decoration on a surface made by pressing small pieces of colored glass or stone into a soft material that then hardens to make pictures or patterns.

myth: A story that was told by a people to explain a practice, belief, or natural event.

punish: To make someone suffer for wrongdoing.

quarry: A place where large amounts of rock or stone are taken out of the ground.

revenge: To harm someone in return for harm done.

sacrifice: To offer something as a way of honoring a god.

version: A form of something that is different from others.

FOR MORE INFORMATION

BOOKS

Bajtlik, Jan. *Greek Myths and Mazes*. Somerville, MA: Candlewick Studio, 2019.

Banville, Sarah, and Quinton Winter. *Monsters: 100 Weird Creatures from Around the World*. London, UK: Wren & Rook, 2021.

Ward, Marchella, and Sander Berg. *A Journey Through Greek Myths*. London, UK: Flying Eye Books, 2020.

WEBSITES

HelloKids: Minotaur Puzzle

www.hellokids.com/c_27502/free-online-games/kids-puzzles-games/greek-mythological-figures-puzzle-games/minotaur-puzzle-for-kids

Test yourself by putting together this Minotaur puzzle.

Kiddle: "Minotaur Facts for Kids"

kids.kiddle.co/Minotaur

Take a look at some of the Minotaur artwork people have made over the years.

The Minotaur's Labyrinth Escape Room

www.warwicklibrary.org/teens/events/13613/teen-virtual-escape-room-minotaurs-labyrinth

Play as Theseus and solve puzzles to defeat the Minotaur and find your way out of the labyrinth. Ask an adult for help if you get stuck!

Publisher's note to educators and parents: Our editors have carefully reviewed these websites to ensure that they are suitable for students. Many websites change frequently, however, and we cannot guarantee that a site's future contents will continue to meet our high standards of quality and educational value. Be advised that students should be closely supervised whenever they access the internet.

INDEX